POSITIVE THINKING

Powerful Secrets to Shift Your Thoughts From Negative to Positive

Robert S. Lee

Contents

Introduction

You are now entering an adventure of exploring
your mind, turning on the positive switch
inside you and dispelling any hint of negativity
to achieve a better you and a happier life.

Hundreds of studies have already proven that our
minds dictate how we react to stimuli, respond to life's
challenges and dictate how we can have happier
existences.

Are you always depressed? Stressed out? Or are
you simply unhappy? Do you want to change
the dark cloud of a mind that you have? If yes,
then you are lucky, because this book is
intended for individuals who want to change
their lives by changing their mindsets into a
positive course.

We cannot eliminate trials or stressors since these are simply part of our daily existence, but millions of people tend to wallow in these negative pit stops in their lives. So, it is my goal to hand over the in-depth knowledge on how harboring negativity will greatly affect you and how choosing a positive disposition will improve your quality of life.

You might be sabotaging not only your mind, but your physical health, mental health and, of course, your happiness by entertaining negative thoughts and letting them prevail. This book will help you win the fight against negativity.

We will focus on the things that we can control. This book will teach you how to regulate your reaction to negative stimuli and manage your emotions and responses.

By the end of this book, you will realize that you are the gatekeeper of your mind. You have the power to transfigure any negative thoughts into positive ones. You will be surprised how changing your outlook will have a ripple effect in attaining a better and brighter life.

Chapter 1. The Power of the Mind

How do you visualize your life? Or rather, how do you want your life to be? You most probably desire a life that is void of stress, conflicts or any untoward incidents.

You may wish or dream about that "perfect" happy life, but do you honestly believe that you can achieve it? Can you really clearly visualize your dream and at the same time have a clear idea of how you can realize that dream?

Most people dream and imagine, but they stop there. They do not realize that any dreams (as long as they are in the bounds of reality) can be achieved only if you put your mind into it.

The mind is a powerful gift. Having a clear mental image of our goals will point us in the right direction. Having a strong mindset will help us mold our attitudes, behaviors, expectations and actions.

Our minds are not linear. We are presented with choices, usually between a positive course and a negative course depending on how we think. This is another gift to human beings. Our mind plus our choices will ultimately become the keys to reaching our goals and dreams.

There is a correlation to things, for example, one action may be a direct effect of one formed thought. As a Chinese proverb says, *"Be careful of your thoughts, for your thoughts become your words. Be careful of your words, for your words become your actions. Be careful of your actions, for your actions become your habits. Be careful of your habits, for your habits become your character. Be careful of your character, for your character becomes your destiny"*. If you try to dig deeper to this adage, you will see the correlation of things and again, how our thoughts or mindsets can affect our entirety.

Multiple studies across different disciplines have proven over and over that our minds are potent and can affect our whole being. Through our thoughts, attitudes, habits, moods and mindsets are born.

Some people are not able to harness the power of the mind, and let the environment or other people control what they think. Instead of forming their own thoughts and goals, they just go with the flow and allow the external factors to create the outcome. The power of choice is diminished and letting a situation or people control the outcome becomes a force of habit.

But like any habit, this can be broken and a new set of habits can be formed. We will be able to "train" our thoughts to embrace positive thinking if we want to succeed in the game of life.

If you want to take the reins and control your life, it is important that you embrace the importance of having a strong positive mindset. This will help you take the right path, the right decision and the right attitude in facing whatever life may throw at you. Remember that

a negative thought will never yield to positive
results.

Chapter 2. The Effects of Negative Thinking

Have you heard the old saying *mind over matter*? It may have different connotations for different individuals, but its root concept is stressing the power of the mind in how we react or handle any given situation, whether it is an experience of pain, fear, weakness or more.

This saying is also applicable in controlling one's thoughts, in the sense that in any given stimuli, we hold the key to how we are going to react.

We ended the previous chapter with a reminder that negative thoughts would not yield any positive results. This is a universal truth. Our mind is a powerful tool that greatly affects our whole being.

In any situation, the way you think will dictate your actions. For example, someone bumps into you, and because of that, your briefcase falls down and your paperwork is scattered in the hallway. A pessimistic person will most likely start to shout, have a higher than the normal BP rate, and may even pick a fight with the person that accidentally bumped you. Thoughts of "I'm going to be late, "I may have lost some important papers" etc. will take over. After the incident, it will seem as if a dark cloud is over your head and your mood is ruined for the whole day. Negative thinkers will have a meltdown or the earlier situation will cause a domino effect on their day.

A positive thinker will most likely accept the apology, pick the papers and go on with his or her day as if nothing happened. See the difference?

You might think that this is just about a ruined day, but it is deeper than that. Your negative thoughts have controlled you, your mood, how you relate to others and even your health and mental state.

Another effect of negative thinking in the field of medicine is labeled as "nocebo" effect or the evil twin of placebo effect. The following example will clearly show how powerful our thoughts can be. Someone was given a diagnosis that he only had a 40% chance to live due to a fatal disease, but given the right treatment he could survive. Physicians usually want to give a clear picture of your health status, but depending on how it was delivered or received, it can potentially lead to negative outcome. If a patient is a pessimist, he will choose to believe the 60% chance of dying, instead of holding onto the 40% chance to live. Instead of following proper treatment, the patient can reject any advised treatment or may continue the treatment with a low spirit. You know the possible outcome for people who lost have their desire to live. And this once again is the power of the mind. You can convince yourself to wallow on negative thoughts and ultimately die.

Here are some of the effects of negative thinking, which will make you reconsider the way that you think:

Physical health- We have established that our thoughts are related to different aspects of our being, one of which is our health. Emotions or feelings are affected by our thoughts can in turn cause health problems. Negative emotions that stemmed from negative thoughts, such as hopelessness and depression can upset our body's hormonal balance and even deplete the chemicals needed by the brain to feel happiness. This has an adverse effect on the immune system that will lower down your defenses.

Negative thoughts can also result in lower energy and stamina.

Repressed anger, caused by poorly managed thoughts, can also bring a wide array of health conditions such as cardiovascular diseases, hypertension and even digestive disorders.

If our system is full of negative beliefs and thoughts, then our body will produce harmful cortisol and epinephrine.

Emerging studies also suggest that some illnesses can also be traced to emotional patterns. These patterns are again affected by our flow of thoughts.

If you are health conscious, then one step in achieving your optimal health is through clearing your mind of negative thoughts.

Emotional downhill –Negative thinking produces negative feelings such as anger, anxiety, frustration, irritability and more. We know for a fact that these emotions should be eliminated, since prolonging emotions such as these can cause a bigger problem such as depression.

Negative social atmosphere- Your thoughts, emotions and actions affect other people. We release a certain vibe into others when we are thinking negatively. Remember that your thoughts can become your words and actions. You can be withdrawn, argumentative or even wary of other people.

Law of attraction– When we are thinking negatively, we simply cannot attract positive elements that may help us get out of any unwanted situations. The state of our mind attracts negative emotions and even events. This is the concept of the Law of Attraction, wherein what you attract in your life are the things on which you focus. If you focus on the negative, then expect negative events to happen. If you are thinking that you are going to fail and experience hardship, then most likely this is what you will get. Your negative attitude will affect your confidence, performance and other elements necessary for you to be successful. You manifest what you think. You might not even notice, but your thoughts also draw similar kinds of people. Two negative thinkers will most likely not result in a positive-inducing relationship. If you fill your mind with negative thoughts, then expect that worries and stress will be your best friends.

Limiting your options – For example, there is a project given to you by your boss and due to time constraints, it triggers your negative thinking and you feel stressed out. Since you keep on thinking that you will not be able to finish your task list, you will soon realize that you lost precious time and energy stressing out instead of actually starting. When you think negatively, your brain actually blocks possible options and choices of how you can go about the projects or any other given situation. What you focus on is the fear of failing and stress. And in the end, your fear is a reality.

Waste of time- To put it bluntly, you are wasting your time by thinking negatively and letting dark emotions associated with this way of thinking overwhelm you. Why be negative if you can embrace the positive side of things? Why be unhappy, depressed, and angry if you can simply be happy? With all the effects of negative thinking to your health, emotions, and social interaction with others, you know that you have to make immediate changes. There is always a better alternative and that is to have an optimistic mind.

How would you know if you are generally a negative thinker? According to the Mayo Clinic, here are ways to identify a negative thinker:

- Filtering – You choose to magnify a negative aspect of the situation and filter out all the good things that happened. An example is that you made a great article, but had a few misspellings. Instead of focusing on the good points of your article that were commended by other people, you focus on the errors that you made and forget the positive points.

- Personalizing – You are most likely familiar with this one, wherein when something bad happens, you put the blame in your shoulders. For example, your boyfriend cheated on you, instead of recognizing that you are a victim, you automatically blame yourself and consider yourself the reason that the relationship did not work out.

- Catastrophizing – If you are chronic worrier, then this will apply to you. You tend to anticipate the worst instead of hoping for the best. If something bad happens at the start of your day, you will start to think that the rest of the day will also be bad, and it will probably will, since your thoughts dictates your mood and actions.

- Polarizing – You categorize things as only good or bad, no in-between. For example, regarding an event that you organized, you either consider it a total failure or great. There are no thoughts of "it went smoothly or it went okay." And if you categorize it as a failure, you will beat yourself up for not being perfect.

If you identify yourself in those four indicators, then you know that it is time to make a change. You have also learned the negative effects of a pessimistic mindset that can greatly affect the course of your life. Do you want to continue to harvest those bad effects? Or do you want to change your life and choose the positive path? Hopefully the next chapter will convince you to move into a much more positive direction.

Chapter 3. The Benefits of Becoming a Positive Thinker

We cannot control external factors in our lives, but we can control the way we think and how we react. Our thoughts will determine how we will deal with whatever obstacles that may come in our way. And I guarantee you, choosing the positive mindset will help you have a better disposition and a happier life.

Here are the benefits of becoming a positive thinker:

Your health- According to the Mayo Clinic, the health benefits of positive thinking are: reduced risk of death from cardiovascular diseases, lower rate of depression, lower levels of distress, and greater resistance to common colds, better psychological and physical well-being and increased life span.

Another added benefit of being a positive thinker is having a better quality of sleep. A good sleep has tons of benefits for the body and the mental state.

Cope better with stress –Positive thinking does not mean that there are zero problems, but it means that you can cope and recover more easily, while at the same time you are able to look at a brighter side of any situation. For example, let's say your presentation failed. If you are an optimist, instead of dwelling on your failure, you know that there are still other chances and you will devise an action plan to correct your errors. But if you are a pessimist, you will just simply give up and paint a negative picture of yourself and think that there is nothing that you can do. To quote Winston Churchill, "A pessimist sees the difficulty in every opportunity; an optimist sees the opportunity in every difficulty."

A positive thinker will also most likely be resilient and be able to face any problems that will come his or her way. Positive thinking will be your shield or coping mechanism to prevent falling into frustrations or depression.

Better relationships –People who are optimistic tend to focus more on the good aspects of people, thus they are more satisfied with their relationships.

Since you also have a better disposition, you will radiate a positive vibe to other people and can infect them with your happiness and uplifting spirit. This will make people want to be in your company.

Better skills – Positive thinking will lead you to strive to develop your skills and develop your resources that can be used later in life. Instead of just giving up, optimists believe that they can be able to rise and actually be better than before.

Greater self-esteem –Self-esteem, as defined by psychologists, is a person's overall sense of self-worth or how one values himself. If you think negatively, you also tend to think of yourself poorly and whenever faced with life's issues or any form of stress and anxiety, you will easily put yourself down and believe that you cannot handle the situation. In contrast, when one has a positive self-image then it also follows that one can make better decisions, assess situations, solve problems, and generally live a healthier and fuller life.

More productive at work - As Collen Barret said, "Work is either fun or drudgery. It depends on your attitude. I like fun." A positive mind is your ultimate weapon that will not only help you enjoy work more but even help you succeed. When you become optimistic, your working attitude will change from dealing with the usual stress at work, criticisms from your boss, or even draining colleagues. You will soon find out that you are able to work more (free from distractions of negative thoughts) and even find ways to be more efficient because you believe that you can do anything that set your mind to. A positive mind can also lead you to the road to success, because your mind will also be more open to possibilities. You will believe in yourself and develop a great working attitude. These are key elements to success. Your promotion is definitely within reach if you will keep up the positive can-do attitude.

Peace of mind- Peace of mind is something that money cannot definitely buy. In order to achieve this, your thoughts should be positive and all negative thoughts and energy should be released. Optimistic people know how to let go of anger, disappointments, fears and essentially all negative thoughts. Remember that no negative thought will result in peace and happiness. Having peace of mind will also result in inner happiness that will surely radiate in you.

Another effect of having a positive mind is being more inspired, appreciative and energized to face tasks.

Do not mistake positive thinking for looking at life through a rose-colored glass. This only means that we do know the reality, but choose to see the better side of things. We know that we can't control everything, so we focus on what we can control, such as our thoughts, emotions and actions. It is having the ability to make the most out of any situation and emerge victorious in whatever life may throw at you. Positive thinking is about choices, being happy instead of sad, being calm instead of mad and smiling courageously instead of weeping in defeat.

Sometimes it seems easier to just give up and think negatively, especially if things seem to not go our way, or if our pictured "perfection" is hard to attain. But in the end, ask yourself if you are happier that way. Always remember the good benefits that positive thinking can bring to your life and how it can affect the people around you.

If you are a negative thinker, but are willing or open to change, then do not fret, the next chapter will help you transition into becoming an optimist. A better you awaits!

Chapter 4. Tips to Overcome Negative Thinking and Become a Positive Thinker

An optimist knows the reality of life, but chooses to focus his or her energy on the brighter side. It is like a choice between a half-full and a half-empty glass—a matter of disposition or way of thinking.

The next steps that you will read are not a walk in a park, especially at first; but you can definitely do it! The more that you exercise the positive way of thinking, the more it will be a part of your system. It is a conscious decision that you will go through every day, but nothing else will yield to a better result in your life. Actress Patricia Neal said, "A strong, positive mental attitude will create more miracles than any wonder drug." This pertains not only to physical aspect, but also tour mental, social and psychological aspect.

Here are some ways on how you can overcome negative thinking and become a positive thinker:

Tip #1: Evaluate yourself (honestly) – You can do this by meditating or having a quiet me-time. You have to identify your usual negative thoughts and from they come. You have to be specific on what area of your life is most affected by your negative thinking. Is it about the way you look, your work, or your romantic relationship? Once it is identified, you have to again reflect and think if beating yourself up or thinking negatively about the situation will help dispel any issues. Ask yourself if your negative thoughts are helping to better the situation. If your answer is no, then the next step is crucial. You have to think of a way to change the situation. Positive thinking calls for an action, not just simply giving up wallowing in a situation. As you begin to practice necessary actions, you will most likely see the results and be inspired to move forward.

It is not a matter of developing an ego, but it is believing that you can further improve yourself and attain whatever you put your mind to.

Tip #2: Squash the negative small voices – With this, you have to be in tune with your thoughts and emotions. When you start to hear your inner voice that tells you that you are not good enough and will not succeed, you have to catch yourself and again meditate and find the positive view of the situation. Another technique is to develop positive statements to replace the negative thoughts that you are entertaining. Change your "I can't" to "I will."Erase words like stress, anger, depression, jealousy, etc. and lean more toward happy, peaceful, loving, motivated, etc. Do not forget that your thoughts become words and actions.

Remember that this is about choices and a matter of self-control. Do not give in to the voice that wants you to be hopeless, helpless and stressed-out. You know that you can do it. You just have to be proactive in dealing with life's challenges.

Tip #3: Ask for help –It is never bad to ask for help from your loved-ones or to seek professional help, especially if you are experiencing major breakdowns, insecurities and other negative emotions that are leading you to self-destruct. A professional can also help you find out the origin of your actions or negative thoughts and, at the same time, can direct you towards healing your heart and mind. Yes, change will start with you, but sometimes, recognizing that you have a problem, knowing its magnitude and sharing it with other people that you trust can definitely help you. There are times that what we need is just reassurance from another person to make things better.

Tip #4: Practice self-affirmation- While we usually want to hear affirmations from other people and even define oneself with their comments or views about us, we have to be grounded in the sense that we know who we really are and, of course, in our self-worth. Sometimes we also have to say "I can do it! I can do this!" -- Even when you don't really believe that you can, by repeatedly saying it with conviction, you will soon realize that you really can do it. Have your own "magic" statement or a mantra. It can "trick" your mind to actually believe in it. Repeat it over and over, or you can also write the positive thought or say it out loud.

Tip # 5: Work on your self-esteem–Some people may appear confident, but can be really unsure of themselves inside. There are times that you have to project a confident persona, and until you make it, make sure that you take the necessary steps to boost your self-esteem. Having a positive self-image will help you eliminate any possible negative thoughts. Here are some ways/exercises that you can use to help you develop this aspect:

This exercise will not touch on any negative views that we might have about ourselves. All you have to do is write down your positive traits and achievements (don't be shy), no matter how big or small it may be. You can also ask your loved ones to add to the list and simply accept that the words written by them are true. Then READ it often especially if you are feeling a bit down. These things should define you, not your fears or failures.

Another exercise is to have "self-esteem check-list."Just simply write things that could make you happy, and then commit to doing these things more often. Or you can be even more specific and plan to do at least one from the list every day. By doing so you are conditioning your mind that you are capable of achieving your goals.

You can also work on your identified weaknesses so they may eventually become strengths.

Tip # 6: Be at your best always - Giving your best shot will make you feel good about yourself and, at the same time, you are giving your self-esteem a healthy boost. For example, you have a presentation at your office. It may be part of your regular meeting only. However, by delivering a presentation wherein you have done your best, not only will you be confident with your work, but other people will surely notice it. Don't be surprised if you receive good feedback (write it down!) and that, in turn, will add more to your confidence level.

Tip #7: Move your body! – Moving your body like exercising and engaging in physical activities can improve your mood. Exercise will not only make your body healthy, but it will also help your mind and emotions to function better. In addition, exercises like yoga can also help release negative energies inside us. They will clear our mind and give us additional strength to face any trials that may come our way. You should couple exercise with healthy food and proper nutrition.

Tip #8: Develop a sense of gratitude - This is a must for everyone if you want to change your perspective into a healthier one. You have to learn to fully recognize and appreciate the good things in life. Why? Your sense of gratitude will feed your feelings of satisfaction and increase your optimism. Why choose to be sad, depressed or agitated when you have all the things in life that you can be thankful for?

Let's try this simple exercise. Develop your "list of gratitude." Just jot down everything in life that can bring you happiness, or the things that you appreciate (even simple things like the beautiful sky that looks like a perfect canvass). Continue adding to the list. At the end of the exercise, you will surely realize that life is good and pessimistic ideas should have no room in your thoughts.

Tip #9: Face the reality that you are not perfect, but can be a better version of yourself - You have to know and understand that no matter how great you are, how stable your life may seem, there will be times that you will have to face problems that can make you fall apart. But the important thing here is that you also know that if you "survive" this phase, then you will come out to be a better version of yourself. So you have to hold on, think of a solution and be patient. This is also closely connected to developing your self-esteem, wherein you will push yourself to achieve your maximum potential.

Tip #10: Do not be too hard on yourself – Sometimes, we are our own worst critics, so you have to work on that. Our self-criticism can cause the flow of negative thoughts and even be the reason for our breakdowns. You have to celebrate every small victories and achievements, and if faced with problems, make sure that your assessment of the situation is not exaggerated or based on emotional thinking.

Instead of saying, "I studied my lessons, but I think I will still fail," say "Let's see what happens when I do my best and what I can do for my next step." Or "I may not be good at this, but with practice I can do so much better."

Clean up your negative statements and learn to refocus. Do not be too hard yourself. You should be your self's biggest fan.

Tip #11: Don't always take things personally – This is one of the characteristics of a negative thinker: automatically blaming oneself for bad things that are happening and be frustrated and depressed by them. Reality check: The world is not all about you. You have to understand that you cannot control how others may think or act, but you can control yourself. You also have to accept other people's individuality that dictates their actions. Instead of getting easily frustrated, try to be in other people's shoes or think of possible reasons for their actions instead of flatly blaming yourself.

Tip #12: Choose rational thinking over emotional reasoning – Closely related to not taking things personally, you have to undo the habit of emotional reasoning as this is highly illogical and will make you feel worse. In every situation, you have to think things through before reacting to them. Do not base your belief on feelings alone.

One should also be more factual in dealing with stressful events or accept the reality, but at the same time look for a solution. For example, "The event that I handled could have been better, but it is not that bad," followed by "Next time I plan to do this...so that it will be successful." By doing this, you are choosing to learn from your mistakes, instead of irrational reasoning that will only further put yourself down. Another golden lesson for this is that there are times that we simply have to accept the things that we cannot change, shut down the negative thinking and move on.

Another trait to learn in order not to be overwhelmed with emotional reasoning is to be a determinist. This means that you understand that a behavior or experience has a cause and effect and not just because of irrational or gut feelings. For example, you feel that you will have a bad day, but there is no logical reason behind it, it may be just triggered by a bad incident earlier in your day. Erase the thought immediately and don't let that thought define your day.

Tip #13: Turn your "what ifs" into actions – You have to learn to face your fears. For example, you fear that you may lose your job, you may entertain your worst-case scenario, but again, you have to be proactive and think of a solution if it happens, or how to prevent it from happening by reinventing yourself. Let go of the fear, as it may cripple you. You may not notice this, but sometimes, your fear is acting out, your anxiety is showing and, in effect, you are not working the way that you should be and will indeed lose the job in the long run. If you have lost your job, then remember that our failures do not define us, but what defines us is the way we stand, face our obstacles and have a better version of ourselves.

Tip # 14: Stop over thinking – It is easy to be caught up with our fast-paced existence, but do not forget the essentials in your life. Remind yourself of the things that are valuable. Always think positively and enjoy life's precious moments and again, do not over think. Give yourself a breather. Have a goal, but do not waste your time worrying over uncertain things. Instead, rejoice over the littlest triumphs and learn from every mistake.

Tip # 15: Learn to be open to change- Sometimes our negative thoughts stem from not being open to change. Instead of welcoming and facing the changes in our lives, we react by fearing the unknown. What we do not understand is that we should take what we can get with every new situation. It is normal and okay to feel a little fear or discomfort, but if you let that fear to get the best of you and control you, then you are keeping yourself from growing, evolving, and reaching your potential. Change is inevitable, but you are also designed to cope with change. It is just a matter of mindset.

Tip #16: Positivity through music- Have you heard the saying that "music heals the souls?" This is definitely true since music can help alter your mood and flow of thoughts. During a negative bout, you can listen to tranquility-inducing music, inspiring music or even an upbeat song if you are feeling a bit down. Stay away from sappy love songs, songs that can make you cry or "noisy" metallic beats that can interfere with your meditation or thinking. Make your own stay-positive music playlist!

Tip # 17: Give yourself a break–

Sometimes, when a situation is so heavy that you can't think clearly, and then you need to "walkaway" from the mess and take a break. By allowing yourself actually to loosen up and enjoy the things in life in a different setting, you are basically helping yourself to de-stress and to reset your mindset, so that when you are finally ready, you have a more fresh and clearer mind to combat life's obstacles.

But take note that even if you are not facing a particular problem, it is a must that you reward yourself from time to time. Spend a day doing the things that make you happy, or spend some quality time with your family and friends. Aside from the fact that you deserve a good break, think of it as a way to fill up your "positivity" container, so that when problems arise or depressions set in, you also have more happy thoughts to get you through the day or simply inspire you.

Tip # 18: Create your own happiness – Pessimistic thinking kills joy. A pessimist tends to define happiness by success, by other people, by the way a situation may turn out, but have you ever thought of who really decides if we shall be happy or sad? The answer is us. This boils down to choice. Our mind is so powerful that we can create our happiness. How? Choose to be happy. Happiness is determined by our thoughts. In whatever situation you may be or whatever stress your environment may bring you, always remember that you have a choice. Choose to be happy and positive.

Tip # 19: Change your mental filter- "When life gives you lemons, make lemonade." This is about the power of changing how we view things. Our minds have a filter, and our habits usually determine how we react to things. How do you transform your mental filter? Here's an example: You are running late and stuck in traffic. Your pessimistic self will most likely start to panic and negative thoughts will run down your mind. This may be hard, but how about accepting the fact that you do not have control over the situation? Why not take the opportunity to chat with your partner? Read an e-book, fix your makeup or pray? Another example: You are in a stressful situation, in which you feel that you are close to a breaking point. Change your mental filter and see that you also have the inner strength to combat the situation, that you have friends or colleagues that will help you through the trying times.

Any situation, it may be bad or good, could be a learning experience.

Tip #20: Pray – This can calm yourself if you are the type of person that has faith in a higher being. If you're not religious, then you can meditate and have your own calming mantra. Tell yourself that you can get through anything. Do not forget that your mind is powerful. You just have to believe in yourself. A positive self-talk can boost your thoughts.

It will all start with a decision of wanting to change, followed by acceptance of your weaknesses and having the self-control to follow the suggested changes in your daily life. Begin with an end in mind, and that is becoming happier and reaching your goals in life through positive thinking.

Chapter 5. How to Remain a Positive Thinker

Many of us know what positive thinking is and the benefits that it brings. Through meditation, affirmation, developed habits, motivation, and self-control, we will be able to achieve positive thinking as an automatic response to any stimuli.

However, it is also a fact that is easier to be positive when things are going our way. During our happy and relaxed time, it is also easier for us to appreciate even the little things in life.

The challenge comes in when real problems or stressful situations arrive. It is easy to fall in a pit, especially when you are just starting or when you have suddenly encountered an obstacle that is too overwhelming. But do not worry, because there are ways in which you can maintain the cup of positivity brimming in your life.

Here are some suggestions:

Regularly check yourself- Have a specific time of the day when you will just stop and evaluate your stream of thoughts. If you find that your thoughts are mostly leaning to the negative, then it's time to give yourself a little shake, a little self-pep talk, and look for ways to put a positive spin to your thoughts.

Have a healthy lifestyle – Exercising and having a good night's sleep can do wonders not only for your body, but these can also clear your mind, making stress easier to manage and having enough energy to face different situations.

Feed your positivity-Find activities that will encourage you to have a more positive image of yourself. You can also find or develop skills that will reinforce positive thinking in your daily life. It may be through keeping a diary, finding a counselor to guide you, meditating, learning calming techniques, reading motivational self-help books and more.

Surround yourself with positive people-Negativity is definitely contagious, but so is happiness. If you seek the company of whiners, needy, demanding people and other individuals laden with this type of trait, you will find yourself picking up their habits and attitude. Plus, your perspective is also altered to match theirs. The company that we choose also reflects what type of person we are. Know the right company for you that will influence your disposition. Surround yourself with people that can bring out the best in you, people that are optimists as well, and people that genuinely care for you and can give sound advice and feedback. Sometimes, you should choose people who can make you laugh and relax your thoughts, since this will help your new-found attitude flourish. Choose wisely.

Work on your pride and ego – Sometimes it is hard for us to let go of things, relax and not be critical of ourselves and others. What the culprit? Our pride and ego. What you do not know is that there is peril if we have a big ego, because instead of focusing on positive thinking, our ego becomes our roadblock. Change will not happen overnight, the important thing is that you are willing to better yourself.

Help other people- No man is an island. Our existence is made meaningful by our experiences and people around us. Make it a point to do random acts of kindness, focus on also helping other people out, especially those people that need a hand to guide them. This will not only make you feel good about yourself, but by genuinely caring for other people, your character is built and a deeper understanding of your personality will also follow. In addition, when you share the positivity within, both you and the people around you will have a positive emotional boost. Radiating the positive emotional and mental attitude should be your goal. As Norman Vincent Peale said, "Change your thoughts and change the world!" Wouldn't that be a better option?

Smile and laugh more often- Aside from the fact that it generally feels good to smile and laugh, it is also scientifically proven that by smiling more often, your overall mood and outlook in life are improved. Laughing more often with family and friends also helps cure the tears and wears that our soul has from negative thinking and emotions. You can smile more often by being with people that you love and care for, appreciating every blessing, doing the things that you like to do.

Rise again- If there comes a day that you fail to focus on the positive, do not be too hard on yourself. After a good cry or a loud scream, rise again and repeat or try all the suggestions. The more that you practice turning your thoughts into positivity the more it will come naturally to you. Remember, you will not be defined by how you fall, but on how you choose to rise in times of trials and adversity. Do not let failure be a hindrance, but instead view it as a learning experience so that when faced with similar situations, you will know how to react and how to cope.

Have a clear vision of what you want for your future – Visualize what you want to achieve, what your goals and dreams are. Think about this every day and create your goals based on that vision. Having a clear vision and a definite goal will create a path for you that will keep you from entertaining negative thoughts. The most important thing, after your visualization, is your actions (set by your goals); do not stop until you reach that goal. You may stumble a few times, but rise again. Keep the fire burning within and carry that vision. Before you know it, you have already become your vision, and a better version of yourself.

Everyone can practice positive thinking. Enjoy the benefits and reverse the adverse effect that negative thinking has brought you. If you ask me if it's possible to stay positive all the time, my honest answer will be no. That is the reality of life; it is not always a ray of sunshine. BUT let me stress this: You can always make your better or positive days outweigh the negative days. Do not let obstacles completely knock you down. As soon as you make that daily choice of always remaining optimistic, then you will soon find out that life is better and happier. You can do it! Believe that you can, and it will happen.

Conclusion

Life here on earth is short, and it should be spent not worrying or stressing about things that come our way. But is also a fact that we live in an era of fast-paced existence, where the world that we live in today is much more complex than that of our forefathers. Life can be so demanding, stressful or hectic that for many, it is "easier" to be disgruntled or stressed or to succumb to tension, instead of consciously choosing to have a positive outlook and attitude. But this mentality should be challenged. There is a better option and that is embracing an optimistic way of thinking.

Our mind is so powerful that our thoughts can influence our words, emotions and actions.

Choosing to let negative thoughts reign in your life w
not only ruin your chances of attaining the best pers
that you can be, but is also distracts you from enjoyi
life's simple pleasures and learning from yo
struggles.

You have to realize that most of the time your
mindset can make or break things. If you want
to succeed in life, be happier and make the
right choices, you have to let go of the
negativity and embrace positive thinking.
Remember that you cannot necessarily control
external stimuli or other people's attitude
towards you, but you are responsible for your
way of thinking and actions.

Hundreds of studies have repeatedly confirmed th
positive thinking generally leads to positive outcom
There are also numerous holistic impacts that we c
enjoy if we choose to embrace positive thinking li
improved health, a longer life span, young

appearance, a peaceful mind, and better relationships for the social aspect. Good self-esteem and healthier coping mechanism is also achievable. It is also known to attract success, happiness, and more.

Do not forget to change your mental filters.
Loss can lead to gratitude; weaknesses can be strengths; tears can be maturity, and failure can be your greatest inspiration. Welcome change as opportunity that can make you a better person. A pessimistic mind will keep you from growing and the sad thing is that if you continue to harbor negative thoughts, then true happiness and peace of mind will never be within your grasp.

If you really want something, if you really want change and to learn how to appreciate more in life through positive thinking, then you have to exert effort and apply the necessary techniques, one step at a time, until you develop the habit.

It may not be easy at first, but it is definitely achievable.

You are the gatekeeper of your thoughts and the master of your fate. You just have to harness the power of having positive thoughts. Create a better world for you and your loved ones. It is all in your hands. You can definitely do it! Good luck with your life's journey! May positivity always dwell in your thoughts!

Thank you and good luck!